TOOLS FOR TEACHERS

- **ATOS:** 0.6
- **GRL:** C
- **WORD COUNT:** 24

- **CURRICULUM CONNECTIONS:** animals, habitats

Skills to Teach

- **HIGH-FREQUENCY WORDS:** are, in, live, mom, the, these, they, what
- **CONTENT WORDS:** babies, bear, climb, cubs, eat, follow, forest, play, sleep
- **PUNCTUATION:** exclamation point, periods, question mark
- **WORD STUDY:** long /a/, spelled ay (play); long /e/, spelled ea (eat), spelled ee (sleep); long /o/, spelled ow (follow); multisyllable words (babies, follow, forest)
- **TEXT TYPE:** information report

Before Reading Activities

- Read the title and give a simple statement of the main idea.
- Have students "walk" though the book and talk about what they see in the pictures.
- Introduce new vocabulary by having students predict the first letter and locate the word in the text.
- Discuss any unfamiliar concepts that are in the text.

After Reading Activities

Encourage children to think of other behaviors they might see bear cubs doing. Invite a volunteer to act out the behavior and ask the other children to guess what the child is imitating. Sound out each word they suggest and ask them to predict the first letter of each before writing their answers on the board.

Tadpole Books are published by Jump!, 5357 Penn Avenue South, Minneapolis, MN 55419, www.jumplibrary.com

Editor: Jenna Trnka **Designer:** Anna Peterson

Photo Credits: Rosa Jay/Shutterstock, cover, 1; Volodymyr Burdiak/Shutterstock, 2–3, 4–5, 16tm, 16bl; guyonbike/iStock, 6–7, 16tl; Jeff McGraw/Shutterstock, 8–9, 16bm; ArCaLu/Shutterstock, 10–11, 16tr; Tony Campbell/Dreamstime, 12–13; Marek Novak/Shutterstock, 14–15, 16br.

Library of Congress Cataloging-in-Publication Data
Names: Nilsen, Genevieve, author.
Title: Bear cubs / by Genevieve Nilsen.
Description: Tadpole (edition). | Minneapolis, MN : Jump!, Inc., (2018) | Series: Forest babies | Includes index.
Identifiers: LCCN 2018005345 (print) | LCCN 2017061700 (ebook) | ISBN 9781624969577 (ebook) | ISBN 9781624969553 (hardcover : alk. paper) | ISBN 9781624969560 (pbk.)
Subjects: LCSH: Bear cubs—Juvenile literature. | Forest animals—Infancy—Juvenile literature.
Classification: LCC QL737.C27 (print) | LCC QL737.C27 N55 2018 (ebook) | DDC 599.7813/92—dc23
LC record available at https://lccn.loc.gov/2018005345

BEAR CUBS

by Genevieve Nilsen

TABLE OF CONTENTS

tadpole
books

BEAR CUBS

What are these babies?

Bear cubs!

forest

They live in the forest.

They climb.

They play.

mom

They follow mom.

They eat.

They sleep.

WORDS TO KNOW

climb   cubs   follow

forest   play   sleep

INDEX